A New True Book

THE NEZ PERCE

By Alice Osinski

Consultant: Mr. Allen Slickpoo, Sr.
Kamiah, Idaho

CHILDRENS PRESS ®

CHICAGO

Nez Perce women with woven, beaded bags

PHOTO CREDITS

Eastern Washington State Historical Society—17

Thomas Gilcrease Institute of American History and Art—38

Idaho Historical Society—39

Image Finders: © R. Flanagan, courtesy Chicago Field Museum—18 (top right and bottom left)

Museum of the American Indian—18 (top left and bottom right), 26 (2 photos)

National Park Service, U.S. Department of Interior—2, 36

Sid Richardson Collection of Western Art—14, 24, 25, 28

© Chris Roberts—Cover, 20 (left), 44 (bottom left)

© James Rowan—6

Royal Ontario Museum—8, 9

The Slickpoo Collection—20 (right), 23, 30 (left), 41 (3 photos), 42 (2 photos), 43, 44 (top and bottom right)

Special Collections Division University of Washington Libraries—13, 34

© Bob & Ira Spring—4, 11 (2 photos), 12, 33

Smithsonian Institution—30 (right)

Washington State Historical Society—21, 31 (2 photos)

Cover: John Conner, traditional dancer, Rocky Boy, Montana

Library of Congress Cataloging-in-Publication Data

Osinski, Alice.
    The Nez Perce / by Alice Osinski.
        p.   cm. — (A New true book)
    Includes index.
    Summary: Describes the history, beliefs, customs, homes, and day-to-day life of the Nez Perce Indians. Also discusses how they live today.
    ISBN 0-516-01154-5
    1. Nez Percé Indians—Juvenile literature. 2. Indians of North America—Northwest, Pacific—Juvenile literature. [1. Nez Percé Indians. 2. Indians of North America—Northwest Pacific.] I. Title.
E99.N5075   1988   88-11822
979.5'00497—dc19   CIP
                                    AC

Childrens Press®, Chicago
Copyright ©1988 by Regensteiner Publishing Enterprises, Inc.
All rights reserved. Published simultaneously in Canada.
Printed in the United States of America.

9 10 11 12 13 14 15 16 17 18 R 02 01 00 99 98

Dedicated to Nez Perce children of the Northwestern United States

TABLE OF CONTENTS

Salmon River near
Whitewater Camp in Idaho

THE LAND
OF WINDING WATERS

Hundreds of years ago
small villages were nestled
in the warm river valleys
west of the Rocky Mountains.
There, along the Clearwater,
Salmon, and Snake rivers,
American Indians had been
living for thousands of years.
These Native Americans
called themselves Nimiipu
(NEE • me • poo), the
Real People.

Explorers
and hunters
traveled among
Native Americans.

When French explorers
arrived in 1805 and saw some
Native Americans with shells
in their noses, they gave them
the name by which they
are known today—Nez Perce
(ness purse), Pierced Noses.
They were divided into two
groups—the Upper and
Lower Nez Perce.

6

SALMON-EATERS

The Nez Perce
lived well in their
rugged country. Each
year, they went on an
amazing journey to gather
food supplies. They
traveled hundreds of miles
on foot or in canoes. They
hunted, fished, and
gathered roots and bulbs.
Dogs were used as pack
animals. Later, the Nez Perce
used horses and were
able to travel farther and

carry more supplies. Food
gathering began in spring.
Bands left their winter
villages near the
mountains and traveled to
their fishing sites on the
rivers to catch salmon.
The Nez Perce were

Nez Perce dried salmon on racks as did many Northwest tribes.

mainly a fish-eating
people. Although they ate
other fish, they depended
on salmon most. After
cleaning the salmon, they
dried and stored it for
winter use. Sometimes ice
caves were used for
storage, too.

HUNTERS AND ROOT-GATHERERS

As the fish supply dwindled, people began to travel to the high country (plateaus) where their favorite roots and bulbs grew. Using sharp sticks, women dug up a root called kouse. After cleaning it, they boiled kouse whole or ground it into a mush. Sometimes they shaped it into small

Blue huckleberries (left) and bitterroot (right)

cakes and dried it for later use. Bitterroot and wild carrots also were collected, as well as a wide variety of plants, berries, and nuts. This was the season of Thanksgiving—Q'eunyit.

The
flowering
camas

By July the bands had
moved farther onto the
prairies to gather the
sweet camas bulb. Nez
Perce from several villages
set up their lodges on the
camas grounds. Other
friendly tribes were invited
to camp with them.

The annual harvest or

By 1900, Fourth of July celebrations marked the annual Nez Perce camas harvest.

food-gathering time was a happy event. People from different bands and tribes shared news and traded things they had made. After hours of root-digging and hunting, people looked forward to intertribal activities, horse races, and ceremonies.

Charles M. Russell's painting depicts
a thrilling buffalo hunt on the plains.

After the camas harvest,
the Nez Perce returned to
the rivers to fish for the
fall salmon. Then hunters
went into the mountains.
They tracked elk, deer,
moose, and bear. Most
hunters returned to their

villages with game. Others crossed the Bitterroot Mountains to the plains. There they joined hunters from other tribes for the great buffalo hunt.

By November most Nez Perce returned to their winter villages. The food gathering was over until spring. Except for small game captured during the winter, families lived on the food they had dried or stored underground in summer and fall.

WEAVING AND HOUSE BUILDING

Nez Perce built several types of dwellings. Some made circular pithouses with flat, earthen roofs. Others built lodges of wooden poles and covered them with woven cattail mats. (Later, buffalo skins replaced the mat coverings.) Often, four or more tipi-shaped lodges were pitched together so

By 1900 reed mats and modern canvas were used in the
construction of Chief Joseph's winter lodge.

that several families could
live comfortably. Summer
houses sheltered families
and drying fish. At root-
digging camps, small,
individual lodges were
built.

Geometric designs were woven into the woman's hat (above) and storage bag (far right). The comb (above right) and buckskin robe (right) were decorated with colorful paint and beads.

The Nez Perce were skillful weavers. They made many woven objects, such as storage baskets, bags, cooking vessels, and horse coverings. Woven hats were worn by the women.

18

GUARDIAN SPIRITS

Like all Native Americans,
the Nez Perce were close
to nature. They believed
that everything in nature is
related. Hanyawat was
the creator. The earth, like
a mother, gave them the
things they needed for life.
And every animal, bird, and
tree was like a relative
to them.

Before becoming an
adult, a young Nez Perce
would go into the

Many Nez Perce would return to the sacred mountain, where they first received their weyekin, to pray and fast for additional favors.

mountains alone to pray and fast. He or she would seek a special guardian (a *weyekin*) for personal protection from danger and for assistance throughout life. The guardian spirit would take the form of an eagle, deer, bear, or some other animal or bird. The *weyekin* would give some people strong powers. These people would become the leaders of the tribe—the doctors (shamans) and war chiefs.

A feast for visiting chiefs given in 1855 by the U.S. government

HORSEMEN OF THE GREAT NORTHWEST

In the 1700s the Nez Perce learned to ride and breed horses. Eventually, the tribe had some of the largest and finest herds in North America.

Nez Perce country was perfect for raising horses. It had rich grasslands and abundant rivers. In winter, the high canyon walls

Nez Perce were excellent riders.

protected the herds from
bad weather.

Families who had large
herds were wealthy. Most
families owned between
ten and twenty-five horses.

Charles M. Russell's painting called *The Brave's Return*

Some had several hundred. They took great pride in covering the horses with beautiful blankets and harnesses that were decorated with colorful paint, beads, and porcupine quills.

TRADING, RAIDING, AND WARFARE

When Nez Perce began hunting and trading with tribes east of the mountains, they discovered new things. Buffalo meat was added to their diet. New items made

On the Great Plains, many tribes fought over hunting rights.

from buffalo bones and skin were used. The Nez Perce clothing and housing started to resemble the styles of the Plains people.

For more than one hundred years, intertribal hunting and trading was

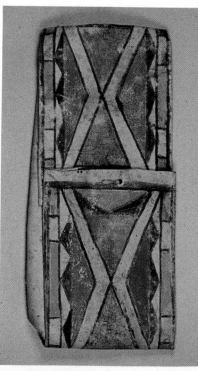

Beaded buffalo robe (above) and painted rawhide container (right)

peaceful. But when some
tribes began trading furs
for British and French
guns, things changed.
Armed raiding parties
made traveling and
camping dangerous. Soon
every tribe wanted guns
for protection. They began
fighting over hunting
grounds.

The Native Americans
desire for European goods
brought many traders into
the Northwest. Soon many
different people were

Miners observing a Native American village

meeting at trading posts. Then missionaries, miners, and settlers began arriving. Forts were built to protect them, and U.S. soldiers were sent to keep the peace. Before long, everyone was fighting for ownership of the land.

A VANISHING HOMELAND

When thousands of settlers began coming into the Northwest, the Nez Perce had problems. How were they all going to live together peacefully?

In 1855 the Nez Perce and other tribes met with leaders of the U.S. government at Walla Walla (Washington Territory). They talked about sharing the land. About 2,500 Nez Perce from different bands

Nez Perce leaders (left) tried to keep peace. However, to protect their families, several of them, such as young Chief Joseph (above), fought.

arrived at the council (meeting). Among their leaders were Lawyer (chosen as head chief by U.S. leaders), Looking Glass, and Old Joseph.

After several days, Native

Lawyer (left) and the
Walla Walla Council of 1855

American leaders agreed to
sign a treaty with the U.S.
government. They promised
to give up part of their
land in the Washington
Territory and move to
reservations where settlers
were not allowed to live.
The government promised

to give the tribes food and blankets, schools, hospitals, and farming supplies.

Few promises made that day by the government were kept, however. In 1860 gold was discovered on Nez Perce land. Miners rushed in without considering the promises of the 1855 treaty. By 1863 Lawyer and other leaders were talked into giving up more land. This time the treaty included the beautiful Snake and

The Sawtooth Mountains and the Salmon River Valley as they look today

Salmon river valleys and the Camas Prairie.

After Lawyer and other leaders signed away lands that belonged to the Lower and Upper Nez Perce bands, they moved to the Lapwai reservation in what

Nez Perce camp at Nespelem, Washington, about 1900

is now Idaho. The Nez
Perce who were against
the treaty refused to leave.
But when more settlers
began arriving in their
lands, the government
forced all of the Nez
Perce to move.

"I WILL FIGHT NO MORE FOREVER"

In the summer of 1877, the Oregon Nez Perce started out for Lapwai. But they never arrived. A skirmish between some settlers and a few Nez Perce developed into a war with the U.S. Army.

Trying to escape the army, the Nez Perce who were against the treaty fled east and then north. They headed

A Nez Perce holds the traditional war pole.

for Canada where they knew the army would not follow. During the next four months, they traveled more than 1,200 miles across rugged country. Several times soldiers caught up

with them. But each time
they fought and escaped.

At the end of September,
the tired band stopped near
the Bear Paw Mountains
in what is now Montana.
They were only thirty miles
from the Canadian border.
As they rested, the army
surrounded them. For five
days the Nez Perce fought
the soldiers. Finally, on
October 5, 1877, the Nez
Perce surrendered.

Before surrendering to Colonel Nelson Miles (above), Chief Joseph had led his people through the Bitterroot Mountains, twice across the Rocky Mountains, through Yellowstone National Park, and across the Missouri River.

Chief Joseph spoke for his people. "Our chiefs are killed...," he said. "It is cold and we have no blankets. The little children are freezing to death... From where the sun now stands, I will fight no more forever."

Although they were taught American ways, Nez Perce
children at the Lapwai school in the early 1900s
played with their own dolls and tipis.

After the war, these
Nez Perce were taken
to Indian Territory in
Oklahoma. Later, they
were sent to the Lapwai
or the Colville reservation.
They were forced to learn
a new way of life.

MODERN LIFE

Nez Perce are proud of their rich heritage. They were the first Americans. Their strong native traditions are an important part of their modern way of life.

Today, most Nez Perce still live on reservations in Idaho and Washington. Although some enjoy modern housing

Each generation of Nez Perce
is proud of its native
traditions

Children begin to learn about their culture at an early age.

conveniences and good education, most families are poor because few jobs are available.

To find work, many Nez Perce have moved away

Close family ties
have always been
an important
part of
Nez Perce life.

from reservations. They live
in cities or near industrial
areas where they can work
on the land that once
belonged to their ancestors.

They drive logging trucks
and work in sawmills near
the forests surrounding the

More than a hundred years ago, chiefs of the Nez Perce nation made decisions with the future of their people in mind. Today, every Nez Perce American builds on the past and looks to the future with pride.

reservations. Others fish on the great rivers. Some have good office jobs.

Wherever Nez Perce live and work, they continue to preserve their history, their beliefs, and their unique traditions. This is a vital part of who they are today and what they and their ancestors have contributed to the spirit of America.

WORDS YOU SHOULD KNOW

annual (AN • yul) — coming every year

bitterroot (BIT • er • root) — a plant with edible roots and pink flowers

breed (BREED) — to produce offspring

camas (KAM • us) — a plant of the lily family with edible bulbs

cattail (KAT • tail) — a plant with a long, brown furry top

council (KOWN • sil) — a group of people called together to discuss problems

cycle (SYE • kil) — action that repeats itself in the same order every time

endurance (en • DOO • rence) — ability to withstand hardship or difficulty

guardian (GAR • dyin) — person who takes care of another

harvest (HAR • vist) — gathering in of food crops

Hanyawat (HAHN • yah • wawt) — Nez Perce name for the creator of the universe

kouse (KOWSS) — an edible root

lodge (LAHJ) — a type of dwelling

missionary (MISH • un • air • ee) — person sent on a religious mission

Nez Perce (NESS PURSE) — tribe living in what is now Idaho, Washington, and Oregon

plateau (plat • OH) — flat land in the mountains

Q'eunyit — "Root feast" held in the early spring — Nez Perce Thanksgiving time

raid (RAYD) — sudden attack

reservation (rez • er • VAY • shun) — land that has been set apart for a special purpose

shaman (SHA • min) — Native American who is skilled in curing illnesses, spiritual leader

skirmish(SKER • mish) — a small fight

sturgeon(STER • jun) — a large fish with rough skin and rows of
   bony plates

supernatural(soo • per • NATCH • rul) — not natural

trappings(TRAP • ingz) — ornaments

treaty(TREE • tee) — a formal agreement or promises made
   between nations

weyekin(WAH • yuh • kin) — Nez Perce word for a guardian spirit

INDEX

About the Author

Alice Osinski has had a varied career in the field of education. Her accomplishments include teacher consultant, director of bicultural curriculum and alternative education programs, and producer of educational film strips. A seven-year teaching experience with the Oglala Sioux of Pine Ridge, South Dakota, and Pueblo and Navajo of Gallup, New Mexico, helped to launch her career in writing. Ms. Osinski has written several articles about the unique life-style of Native Americans. Her previous books in the New True book series include The Sioux, The Chippewa, The Eskimo, and The Navajo.